The Prettyboys of Gangster Town

Martin Grey

First published September 2020 by Fly on the Wall Press
Published in the UK by
Fly on the Wall Press
56 High Lea Rd
New Mills
Derbyshire
SK22 3DP
www.flyonthewallpoetry.co.uk

ISBN: 9781913211240
Copyright Martin Grey © 2020

The right of Martin Grey to be identified as the author of this work has been asserted in accordance with the Copyright, Designs and Patents Act 1988.

Typesetting and Cover Design by Isabelle Kenyon.
Cover Image: Shutterstock

A CIP Catalogue record for this book is available from the British Library.

For the friends and family who didn't make it this far.

The world is a poorer place without you.

Praise for The Prettyboys of Gangster Town

"Martin makes the ordinary extraordinary, turns the mole hill into the mountain."

- Sophie Sparham, Performance Poet

"The Prettyboys of Gangster Town is an open-hearted, compassionate debut collection from Martin Grey. These poems are wistful, warm and highly emotionally-engaging, articulating the joys and pitfalls of modern life from a number of different perspectives, while always remaining true to Grey's distinctive poetic style. There are some real gut-punches in this collection too - all life is laid bare with a beautiful eye for the detail- but at its heart, this is a book all about empathy."

- Leanne Moden, Poet and Performer

"If there is one central force which pulses through the words of Martin's work, it is love. In spite of life's let downs and losses, love is discovered and cherished on a rite of passage from a grubby nightclub and teenage dreams to handling the daily bewilderments of attempting this thing called adulthood. Get ready for love as big as any astronaut's favourite planet. There is enough love between these pages to start a revolution. These stanzas brim with love for the melody of lyrical language, subtle internal rhyme and imaginative wordplay. This book also enthusiastically explores boy-meets-girl love, without saccharine or cliché, but with gen-uine openness at the awkwardness and potential highs of trying to navigate an optimistic heart. On top of all of this, you will be subjected to some very important questions, such as 'does anyone like their knee caps' and 'is it OK to dunk a custard cream?' (The answer to the latter is 'No'). A relatable, hope-raising read for both the realist and romantic."

- Dominic Berry, winner of Saboteur 2020
Best Spoken Word Artist

CONTENTS

Bones

Ding.

The remnants of her yellowed hair
were too weak to hide her sinkhole cheeks
from the breeze of our approaching night bus.
Her twenty going on cold turkey bones rising
and falling with a moving mouth silenced
by the idling of the engine.
Her worn too often yellow tracksuit is almost two-dimensional
on her stick limbs and twig fingers fumble change against
the hissing open door; the suburban one-am sky.
Eyes falling, pair by pair, as they see her through the window,
into phones with and without battery, writing real and fake
messages of 'don't talk to me'.
Possessions repositioned for maximum 'don't sit here'.

"Please."

Her jagged urgency bouncing off the stop bells and our
shrinking comfort zones,

Ding, four stops,

hitting her bones in waves as she stumbles at the empty
priority seating right in front of me, her moving mouth
silenced by the idling of our conscience.

"Does anyone have change for the bus?
I really need to get home."

Held hushed by her helplessness and the fear on her breath,
my heart in sync with the engine vibration, my hands
unprepared for this situation.

"PLEASE."

Someone finally fumbles and I fumble too, finding a pound
and a penny, telling her *sorry, it's all I have on me.*
Not sorry for the bones and the pity blue veins overpowering
her punctured skin, or that it took two pleas for someone to
break from a phone with or without battery, writing real and
fake messages of 'don't talk to me'.
Her moving mouth silenced by the scorn of the delayed,
acceleration shaking terror from her almost tears as she rests
her stretched and sagging forearms from the back of the seat
in front of me.

When the potholes swing us in unison, I see the bruising in her
malnutrition,

ding,

and every pitfall of our filled up bellies on her bared, yellowed
teeth, but my shrunken comfort zone doesn't let me ask her if
she'll be okay. Three stops.

"I need to pay you back, I need to"
ding,

she fires at me, suddenly, my attempts at kindness bouncing off
the half-unzipped caves where her neck should be,

Ding,

and every time I tell her she doesn't, she fumbles a crumpled ten
or twenty from a pocket at the now hissing open door her other
benefactor quietly departs from, almost one for all the spinal bones
pushing through her top,

ding,
as she saves them from the half-crushed cans on the floor.

Eyes in phones with and without battery see her shove them
all right at me,
ding,
see me close my hands and cover my pockets as if they've seen
this exact scene time and time and time again.
Ding, two stops, I want to stop her, to calm her motion blur, but
I can't move anything in case I accidentally hit her.
Ding,

"Please" I say, *"Keep your money,*
I want you to get home safely".

I want to get home safely and it calms her just enough, just slightly,
but my shrunken comfort zone still doesn't let me ask her
if she'll be okay,
or if she can eat those bones away,
or if home is even a safe place to stay,
ding,
because I don't know what I would do if she told me.

Ding.
Me this time, telling myself that she'll be fine, because my
shrunken comfort zone wants this to stop when the bus does.

Ding,

as she pulls her bones up by the stop bell,
ding,
as if she's getting off too,
ding,
but I don't know how to be alone with her in the street-lit stillness
we've been cutting through,

ding.

"Please," she says.
Ding.
"Can I have a hug?"

I see the worst of myself, when I assume the worst in her,
but I try to wrap my shrunken comfort zone around her bones, tightly
enough to mean something, gently enough to protect me from
her pain and protect her for a moment from the cracks we let her fall
through, but my shrunken comfort zone still doesn't let me ask her if
she'll be okay, as I tell her again to get home safely and head alone to the
dark breeze outside the hissing open door.

My hair too meek to hide my hapless cheeks
from the breeze of her departing night bus.
Her worn too often yellow tracksuit almost too late for her stick limbs.
Her twenty going on frail bones falling and falling with a moving mouth
silenced by downward pairs of eyes,

in phones with and without battery, writing real and fake messages

of 'don't talk to me'.

fish

Fish, Chips, Bread and Butter and a Cigarette

The bus went twice a week back then. A return ticket to Hollywood, from
a stop by the village well, long since succumbed to a housing
development that seemed so modern at the time. The
chippy often got him telling me stories from his
youth, bold and retold memories, deep
fried in my hungry naivety. Him
and his friends, they'd wait
for ages, sometimes.
They had

to get to
the bus stop early,
stare down the road in the
hope it hadn't passed already and
if they were lucky, they'd catch the coal
merchant's bored horse skulking off alone again, or
the rag and bone men looking for a bargain. A far cry from the
far-flung, cinematic worlds of sharp suits and femme fatales awaiting
them after the town centre chippy, a fortnightly tale of its little speciality,

fish, chips, bread and butter
and a cigarette.

In my still-warm fish I'd taste his story, as if the crunch of teeth on
batter could take him back to the bus with me, where the
bright-eyed stars of an old man's tale made him
fifteen again, as it all unveiled. Him, his
friends and I, we'd munch away on
sustenance served in yesterday's
smudged out headlines. He'd
be as black and white

and mid atlantic
spoken

in a

as
the movies
he saw in between
the removable letters above
the foyer door and the black dots flashing
every fifteen minutes, to change the reel once more.
I'd ask him all the questions I never thought to ask him at
the time, with both our lives ahead of us, instead of only mine,

over fish, chips, bread and butter
and a cigarette.

His factory working, water fetching, vegetable picking ways, Sundays to
Fridays and alternate Saturdays, left him just enough for the bus,
food and matinées, but still less than the pocket money not
paying for my still-warm fish, in paper so plain it
became the canvas for stories lost between
then and those days, my still warm
chips the b-feature to a bit
of time with the him
I never knew.

But even
with his world at my
fingertips, I can't access a place
where no history exists, and without his stories
I would never understand the younger days of the elderly
man who bought me still warm fish and chips, all those years
ago, when he ate before movies with pre-war naivety, unaware that
smoking causes cancer, or that some would soon be conscripted forever

from fish, chips, bread and butter
and a cigarette.

It Rained a Lot in Berlin that Day

with the never-ending burble
of a kettle a minute from boiling.
Your delayed arrival
stranding you eight stops from home,
in the U9 flood near Tiergarten.

It rained a lot in Berlin that day.
A one in sixty-year soaking,
keeping the beer drinkers
from benches by the *Späties*.
No street musicians to serenade
the sodden Schönhauser swarms
leaving fewer empty bottles by the bins.

It rained a lot in Berlin that day.
Countless droplets bounced off the tags
and the *Ampelmännchen* leading to the
side streets, where they rarely seemed
to cut the foot-high grass,
while we shared a little laugh or two,
about the surfboard in the Airbnb
you said we wouldn't need again.

It rained a lot in Berlin that day.
A reign of puddles and shoes with holes in,
making it slippy in Einstein Kaffee.
A vodka bottle with a glass or two,
waiting on your kitchen table,
a secret thank you
for letting us crash there,
while you'd been away.

It rained a lot in Berlin that day,
where for once the ubers
were fuller than the ubahns,
but we were more intent
on you getting safely home
than working out another day
to cook for you like we'd promised you,
before sharing a Berliner or two
on your balcony.

It rained a lot in Berlin that day,
but we were drenched in afterglow,
from the *wilkommen* you show us,
every single time we go.

I Should Have Said Something

"Why don't they try speaking English?"
he muttered.
The back of a flat cap
shaking slowly,
as a Polish family
stowed their luggage
a little up the carriage.
A private assumption,
hiding in the background noise
of the train,
as it pulled away
from the airport station.

"Shouldn't be here if you can't speak English,"
she mumbled.
A few flicks of faded hair,
falling through the headrest,
the only clue
to who should be,
or if her case was full
of polyglot mentality,
from a country
where she speaks
the language fluently.

"What annoys me is when they get on with their trolleys,"
he murmured.
"You ask 'em to move their bags and they say no."
I leaned into the gap between us,
at the blotches and wrinkles
in the face below the flat cap,
to ask him what he meant exactly,

bars,

why a family
without a trolley
was making them so angry.

"*Can't do anything yet,*"
she mouthed.
Their closing eyes
nodding with agreement.
My resigning eyes averting
from what she'd want to do,
and when she thought
it would be acceptable to do it,
falling back
into how they'd be deceived
when their problems didn't leave,
after those who *shouldn't be here*
had gone.

I said nothing.

Time Machine

Sometimes, the insides of my eyelids
are a grounded time machine,

tied to the present, by burnt-out wires hanging from the specific date I
entered in the smouldering time selection circuit, and I can't correct the
past until I properly fix it. Every time I try, I recover lots of you-specific

media from shock-damaged parts of the internal memory, so if I could
get back to you, I'd be able to correctly remaster the exact pitch of your
laugh, when we stood outside the local and said we'd meet up soon.

But sometimes, the insides of my eyelids
are metal fatigued.

I couldn't stop the saline lubricant from dripping out the ducts above the
blinking warning lights, and sparking a full system feedback loop on your
birthday, which overloaded the gyro-stabilisers, and stopped me testing

my latest fix by flying to our renovated stamping ground. I could improve
the date-specific durability by rerouting the time selection circuit through
the full closure interface, but I'd need to get a part off you first, and the

Fermi Paradox failsafe would still work perfectly, ready to cloak my
appearance at the time we said we'd meet up soon, no matter what power
tools I take to its impenetrable shell.

Sometimes, the insides of my eyelids
are unfixable,

but I keep the annotated map of our universe by the thruster control, just
in case I ever bodge my time machine and fly right back to our unrenovated
stamping ground, when we said we'd meet up soon. If only for a microsleep,

---

and if I had to rip the seat out, to shed enough weight to compensate for the
crackling wires in the smoking time selection circuit.

Sometimes, I think if I made it back, then I'd secretly tell you how I'd tried
to fix the insides of my eyelids,

before the exact pitch of your laugh
told me I didn't have to.

sky,

She Had Beautiful Hair

with access to the launch codes
for the missiles in my atria,
that unsettled every tingle
of my polluted plasma
when the red-shifted city
distorted distant soliloquy
from her nonchalant certainty
that any future existed only in my veins
and if this proved to be a dream of a life
then all I'd be was platelet insane,
a subordinate to my potential energy
until a blip in my stelliferous era
passed into another state,
where my toxifying circulation
would be someone else's fate.

In our two in billions catching of eyes
of septillionth generation bacteria conspirators
in the interconnections of causality
that raised me up with my chemical reactions,
I imagined a box under all I could see,
knowing the probability of her potential energy
meant she'd probably forever again
be anywhere but inside it,
that in spite of the millions
of years of input and reaction
enabling our blood types to almost coincide,
the ordered energy we sent
and the disordered energy we reflected
only clotted the future of my universe
in the way it was always intended to be.

confusing

The pocketful of heads and fails
I call my best guess at infinity
always knew that, as soon as I let go
of my disordered potential energy,
I'd become kinetic energy
and fall toward the concrete,
to a thud that tells me not to fight,
that when a star dies, I lose more light,
until all I am
is an infinite collection of infinite entropy
full of infinite strings of absolute zero
freed from my weak anthropic excuses
for chemtrails waiting to settle in my veins,
ready for their missiles
to be fired once again.

Focus

I must get this done. Focus.

I'll make a nice cup of tea first. Then I'll focus.

Well, you can't have a brew without a biscuit, can you? I think the shop's got custard creams on special, the ones with the proper structural integrity, where it's possible to munch the four corners into a relatively symmetrical diamond. A little walk might fix my knee pain anyway. Why do knees expand like that when you bend them? Focus. It's like the inner bit absorbs the whole of the knee-cap. I don't like my kneecaps. Does anyone like their kneecaps?

I can't believe my knee gave way at those South Korean prayer stones that were something to do with stopping a small dragon from getting a white ball if you stacked them seven or eight high, otherwise the dragon would get the ball and that was bad. Something like that. I think my photo of the tourist explanation is on the encrypted external hard drive I can't remember the password for. How do you decrypt a hard drive? Why did I even encrypt it? What else is on it? Focus.

I bet my housemate forgot to wash up again. He doesn't even soak his pots, he just leaves them until his formerly *al dente*, now puddle pasta remains are harder than a cyborg Jason Statham, in the third act of a movie, and I've got nothing to cook with. Does he think I'm his cleaner or something? And he's only got those rubbish rich tea rip-offs that spontaneously combust when they get within ten feet of a cup of thirty second brewed Typhoo. Why even buy a biscuit you can't dunk? Champion dunkers, custard creams.

I should get in touch with the Korean woman I met in Seoul. We had a great time at that tearoom where you had to leave your shoes outside. I think we're still Facebook friends, but she's not liked or commented on anything since we met. Unless it's culturally important for me to go first, a bit like how everyone asked me how old I was so they knew how to address me. But then I probably shouldn't have kissed her. Focus. When we were smashed on soju, she must have felt like she was trapped in a malfunctioning car wash, but also didn't back out of it, although she was leaning against a wall. Focus.

She looked amazing in that purple dress. Focus.

Don't check that text. Who sends a text these days? It's probably a few more grand in PPI or whatever compensation from a loan I never had, for some vital approaching deadline I thought had already passed. Maybe I could claim it all anyway, I might end up as the 7,209th richest person in Britain and lose the financial need to get this done.

She could steal military secrets with legs like that. Maybe she is a spy, like one of those Russian spies, except Korean. I'd be rubbish at keeping secrets from a Russian spy. Maybe one of my friends is a spy and she's tracking them through me. Maybe she wants my hard drive. How do you find out if someone's a spy? She might be up for it though, we could sell stolen secrets for a small fortune and scarper to a country with a non-extradition treaty, Brazil never used to have one, or Ecuador, I think that's where Edward Snowden was headed before he got asylum in Russia. Focus. I sort of speak Spanish, that'd be fine, we could open a cafe, call it Cafe de Kimchi or something. We could sell those massive custard creams. Focus.

Says they're all in my local if I change my mind. I can't sip beer in the sun with my mates, I must get this done. Maybe one soft drink. It's only a minute past the shop. A walk would be good for my knee anyway and I do need some custard creams.

Dancefloor

These chords
are ours.
Eight Fs,
seven Gs
and three A minors,
that make us punch our fevered hands
above our frown lines and scream,
before beckoning our abandoned aspirations
back from the scratches
on the Rock City dancefloor,
where our bassline beats
to forgotten bonds
formed in our rites
of four-four passage,
before our riffs became retro.

Before our demo made us rock stars,
with Liam on rhythm,
me on lead,
Dave on bass and vocals,
we'd open for our heroes
on their *Up the Bracket* tours
and Rock City would throng
to our songs every Saturday.

But our unwritten anthems
are as unknown to the Libertines
as their riffs seem to be
to the spartan dancefloor.
A minor, D, G, E minor,
A minor, D, G, E minor,

but we're not allowed to dance
on stage anymore
and no-one jumps around anymore,
you don't need to wear your worst shoes
anymore
and we don't have mates at the zero-deep bar
who sneak us rounds for a quid
anymore,
because the walls are a different shade of black,

and I wish Dave was here.

Because our chorus is coming,
and we wrote down all our dreams
on lost bits of paper,
so we'd always remember
how to hit every note
when we strum the air,
and how to headbang
like before we banged our heads
against our bad attempts at melodies,
spilling beer on the bands
we still emblazon on our hearts
as we embrace in sweat-ridden anticipation
of eight more Fs,
seven more Gs
and three more A minors,

AND WE NEVER REALLY LIKED IT ANYWAY!
SO MUCH PREFERRED IT THE OTHER WAY, YEAH!

This chorus is ours,
and we have reclaimed our dancefloor

---

until our song is over,
shouting out of tune friendships
that saved us from tomorrows
at future gig posters
we're too yesterday to know,
kissing every A minor,
D, G and E minor
we can grab from the mesh
on the speaker cones,
because no-one will ever know
this song,
on this dancefloor,
like we do,

and I wish Dave was here,

because this moment is ours.

So, let's never come back,
and let's never write a song again,
but let's dance like we did
when we fractured Dave's rib
until the very last note of our outro,
and let's sing
like Pete Doherty and Carl Barat
would have proper loved our demo,

even though
we never really
liked it anyway.

Museum

Bulging bags in dingy basements
unsafely stow exhibits I collected
from our best abiding attempts at glories,
carefully numbered, catalogued,
cross-referenced with our future plans
and traded little stories.

I'd miss trying not to miss you,

but in my bright rooms of empty displays
I build your legacies on sorrow;
while my ever-silent audio guides
talk in depth about the yesterdays
you find a way to weave
in my tomorrow.

I'd miss trying not to miss you,

but I curate my ripped-up info cards
in a cordoned off exhibit hall
of artefacts reimagined from within,
slowly losing you in me,
until I admit the entropy
of our eternal spin.

I'd miss trying not to miss you.

The Bad Guys

You said the bad guys will kill us
if we don't kill them first.

Would they kill us with the weapons that we
sold them when they were still our friends?
Would they kill us with the "patriots"
they use to justify their ends?
Would they kill us 'cos we'd kill them first?

You said the bad guys will kill us
if we don't kill them first.

Would they kill us with a million more
with no option but to run?
Would they kill us with the space
between an itchy trigger finger
and praying pairs of eyes
where hope or mercy used to linger?
Would they kill us 'cos we'd kill them first?

You said the bad guys will kill us
if we don't kill them first.

Would they kill us with loaded headlines
that deceive us as they pry?
Or with blind eyes for atrocities
committed by our "allies"?
Would they kill us with the acts their
Gods would not do in their name?
Would they kill us 'cos we'd kill them first?

You said the bad guys will kill us
if we don't kill them first.

Would they kill us with yet another
war to make us "safer"?
Or with the money-making munition
shares stringing us along?
Do you think there's value in a human
life while there's profit in a bomb?
Would they kill us 'cos we'd kill them first?

You said the bad guys will kill us
if we don't kill them first.

Breathing.

If You Were

I wanted to tell you,
I thought you'd like to know,

if you were a Monday morning,
you'd sing a storm so strong I'd skive off
work and watch bad movies with you all day long.

If you were a soft furnishing, you would be a blanket, for
every time you smother me I know I'd be all warm and comfy.

If you were a pencil grading,
you'd be about 4B, for it's *oh so very softly*
that you make your mark on me.

If you were a French audio guide,
I wouldn't understand, but I'd listen to your
melody and know that life was grand,

and if you were a famous landmark,
you'd be the Eiffel Tower,
because I really, really like it.

I hope you don't mind me telling you,
I thought you'd like to know,

if you were a beer, you'd be a limited edition,
multi award-winning trappist beer, where they only brew
a few each year, so every sip is super special.

If you were an electronic device,
you'd be a dictaphone, because I'd be one
if I didn't phone you when I can't be by your side.

Accepting.

If you were a metal detector, you'd never need to start,
for you've already found the keys to my...softer side.

If you were an invention, you'd be a suitcase wheel,
because you always lighten my mind
no matter how weighed down you feel,

and if you were a non-fiction book from the 1980s,
you'd be the Usborne Spotters Guide to Dinosaurs, for as long
as you and I will live, I know you'll give me more and more.

I hope you like me telling you,
I thought you'd like to know,

if you were something that fell in the ocean,
your buoyancy force would be less than 9.8 newtons,
for it's when I sink right into you that I find my equilibrium.

If you were an integral aspect of modern skyscraper design,
you would be the lift, because you don't need
the stares from all those strangers.

If you were a part of your sneeze, you'd be the little
nose twitch you do before achoo, for you would bring me
to my knees if you lost the things that made you you.

If you were a condiment, you'd be a sugar sachet,
for if I ate a lemon, you'd be there for my mouth,

but most importantly of all, if you were a button
on a telly remote, you'd be the big red one, you see,
because no matter where you're taken to,
you always standby me.

Breathing.

We Could Start a Revolution

you and I.

We could harness the hope we think will pass on by in every broken promise, via every street-lit side effect of late evenings in our endless daily grind, as no amount of serotonin can fully hide the unquantifiable fear behind our eyes, the rawness in our rejections, the frustrations in our failures, the melancholy in the missed opportunity we never quite forgot, the regret in what we allowed to drag us down. Or when our friends filled our conversations with fables from every corner of the Earth, while you and I flailed with a dearth of worth, as if it was water in a broken glass.

But we could start a revolution, you and I.

We could make love to our front lines, turn them into a brightened sky, serenade our sorrow, borrow the best from each other's corneas, know that nothing would be nonsensical as we filled each other's trenches and that every piece of inner peace would be pure when we flushed away our finality.

Then we could start a revolution, you and I.

We could teach each other how to fly, to soar above our endless search for perfection, where our lungs harness the photosynthesis in our fingertips as they touch our formerly unreachable sky, our needs nurtured by riches that no amount of money could ever provide and we could learn to share our revolution, so that no-one we care for would ever be thirsty, would ever be cold, and that maybe something we'd say or do would make them want to start a revolution too, because someone, somewhere, made me want to start a revolution with you and we could bask inside our revolution, always as young as the potential we saw in each other's imperfections the first time we met.

We could start a revolution, you and I.

We could inspire everyone with the warmth inside our eyes, until every single child is born with a chance, until every single soldier wants to lay down their arms. If everyone wanted peace, there'd be peace. If everyone wanted to be more, we'd be more. If you wanted to start a revolution too, then we'd recycle hate into cushions for our falls with decent human rights for all, we'd show all the bigots love is not about 'nation', with an end to social deprivation, we'd find cures for every destructive disease by fixing everyone who's bringing our world to its knees, even if we only see the beginning. You might think it's impossible, that I'm deluding myself dumb, but all we'd have to do is be the people we'll become. We could do anything, if we gave it a try.

We could start a revolution, you and I.

The Rain Outside My Window

I hear you,
hammering my window
as hard as you can.
Your intoxicating,
saccharine cry
trying to seduce me.
Trying to drown me.

I do *not* fear you,
if I'm in here
and you're out there.
I'm deafeningly dry
when I listen to you bounce
off the boundary between us,
desperately calling me,
darkening your sky.

I will never ignore you,
or forgive you
for the bludgeoned eyes
and battered ribs
you'd inflict on me
so easily,
for tearing me
from my hiding places,
through the shards of glass
you made me swallow
from every
shattered window,
for the cost
of the quadruple glazing
you tap on.

I make it clear for you,
but you never listen,
not to me,
not to *anybody*.
I see through
every single drop,
and you will never
seduce me
again.
Not now I'm the one
who has control,
of the rain outside my window,
of the pane outside my soul.

Homeless Guy

He's sitting on
the Starbucks wi-fi,
as it leaks into a laptop
in the window by his head.
Staring at the ground.

Homeless guy.
No-one looks him in the eye.
He used to have a dog.
It must have died.
"Spare any change please."
His fading brink
on a filthy din of
"Sorry mate,"
"Get a job,"
why he's even asking.
Someone nearly kicks him,
while they fumble
with a shopping bag.

Homeless guy.
People pass on by,
to their sofas
and their central heating,
as I normally do.
Empty doorway
on the corner,
let now agreed,
keeps him out the
whinge and rain,
unless it's blowing north.

Homeless guy.
I tell myself I shouldn't pry.
He might have lost a wife or kid,
or been sanctioned over nothing.
He might have not been diagnosed,
or been injured in Afghanistan.
I gave him 50p.
I gave myself the illusion
that I live my life compassionately.

Homeless guy.
I didn't look him in the eye.
I didn't mean not to.
I just didn't.
"Thanks mate," he says.
"No worries," I reply.

Homeless guy.
We're not much different,
him and I.
Failed plans,
Illness,
people we miss.
A name.
But

Homeless guy.
He knows my lie,
that a 50p
might change it.

Haematomas

It's been a bruising time.
A sucker punch of circumstance
that put us way off line
and resigned you to nothing more
than little more to lose.
You paint my good intentions
on the discoloured bags
below our bloodshot eyes,
so when I tell you things get better,
you draw my line
in sand already moistened
by advancing tides.

It's been a bruising time.
Your flailing fingers flounder
for what you think we need
to punch-drunk repair ourselves.
I tell you things get better,
but it makes you want to claw
at future plans
that ruptured capillaries
with our compassion.

It's been a bruising time.
It bleeds you almost numb,
but we're kindred haematomas
who'll drag each other on.

Tea and Biscuits

When I couldn't make it better,
she'd make a cup of tea.

A floral pot of remedy
for me against the world,
with a custard cream
to calm my hunger,
resting on a matching saucer
and maybe one for luck,

but no dunking.

Tea and biscuits became compulsory,
as her independence poured
from the spout of her fragility,
but when no amount
of corner shop runs
or carrying the tray
could counteract her cancer
and her cataracts,
she'd make a cup of tea.
A floral pot of remedy
to remember her by.

I'll always put the kettle on,
when you can't make it better.

Escape Velocity

I want to be an astronaut.

I want us to break escape velocity and soar beyond our
atmosphere, from Earth to outer space. I want us to fly
until Madrid to Mount Fuji fit inside our warm embrace.

I want to be an astronaut.

I want us to sit on space debris blowing our anxiety
away, until we see unpolluted skies twenty-four
hours a day.

I want to be an astronaut.

I want us to sail to Mars on solar winds, build castles
in its dark red sand, I want us to jump in its 0.4 of
Earth's gravity as high as we can.

I want to be an astronaut.

I want us to hitch a ride off Halley's Comet, through
the asteroid belt, slingshotting ourselves to Saturn,

where I'd get some rings for your co-pilot fingers
and we'd paint Stephen Hawking's soul on Titan's
orange-blank canvas.

I want to be an astronaut.

I want us to lasso Voyager 2, swing ourselves through
the Kuyper belt towards her, past the spot where her
older sister cocked her head

to *pale blue dot* our insignificance, so we can tell her
she hasn't been forgotten by giving her a hand through
the heliosheath. I want us to push her on

so third law hard we'd launch ourselves back to our
cleaned up Earth with just enough time to shout at
Pluto, *you'll be a planet again!*

and to break through Europa's ice,
to wave at the undiscovered life
in its unexplored liquid methane.

I want to be an astronaut.

Come with me.

We

We nourish our neuroses.
We feature wall our fears.
We pummel our protection
while we ostracise our years.

We mutilate our mercy.
We doctor our denial.
We acidify our souls
while we bask in all our bile.

Rock City

I was desperate for a working time machine; a DeLorean,
a phone booth, didn't matter. As long as it took me back
to the Rock City dancefloor during *Here Comes the Rain*,
when she disappeared to the bathroom, so I could grab the
arm of my younger self and implore him to leave the gig
before she had his number.

When he'd shrug me off and tell me to get lost, I'd tell
him *he* would, between affairs in the few minutes longer
than it should have taken walks to the corner shop, until
she'd walk half a step in front of him to keep an eye on
his eyes, how they'd awkwardly arrange the table mats and
TV remotes to cover up the worst of the gouges, and the
checks on volume, current channel and previous channel
when she arrived back home. I'd put myself between him
and the music to tell him where she'd keep the stolen
medication he'd wash and wash down the sink.

How she'd threaten to stab his eyes while he was sleeping.

And how he'd learn to be silent,
because one hit back would have made him guilty of being
more than the worst of the monster he *deserved* to be.

But when he still wouldn't listen, I'd hurl my feeble fists
at his eyes, ribs, anywhere, until I took a dive when the
bouncers came, smiling wide as we were hauled away,
knowing that being barred from Rock City would be a
price I was prepared to pay.

for your

Slats

I knew you'd be here,
that I'd unclip the lead
around what endures
with your view of our
curving trees and trusted contours.
As if you could look at anything else,
do anything but wait to bask
in bursts of shared experience
on the bench around the corner
from the ageing leisure centre.

I've been waiting patiently
outside your view,
while the woman sat with you
messaged her meal away,
with a half look of recognition
that made me wonder
if they knew you too.
I hope it's nice to be in touch like this,
on slats made of heights as tall
as your upside-down abyss,
where our half-done days
and half-made ways
gnaw at what we'll never do,

but right now,
I'm just hanging out with you.

I've picked up the litter left all around you,
and as best as I could, I've cleaned the dirt
that gets in between your from and your to,
as if preening your plaque whenever I come here
will somehow diminish how much I miss you.

I hear your voice messing gleefully
with how we got through,
and I see you worry when I want to give up
on the future you should've had too.
With grass so green and horizons so wide,
we rest in a place where I learn to confide
in the face you'd have made at becoming a bench,
when you hated so much to be sat on.
I hanker for more than what we'll never do,

but right now,
I'm just hanging out with you.

These moments are constants
I'm trying to show you,
to slow down the entropy
that one day won't know you,
as the goal post in front of our curving trees
makes it less like the view you saw every day,
as, one by one, we move further away.

I don't mean for the splinters in my throat to define you,
I'm just happy for a place where, for now, I can find you,
as I tap you and tell you, *it's great to see you*
and I'm sorry that our future plans turned out the way they did.

The Prettyboys of Gangster Town

"Get yer swank on, mate, get yourself down,
the boys are on their way to G-town.
Be in Yates by eight o'clock
and learn to flirt with the ladies, you Spock."

G was for Guildford. G was for gangster,
and those were the words of our Al Capone
when small town boys sought small town joys,
every Saturday night.

From the Bridge Street bars to Bo's just down,
past every place to be in a three club town,
we'd eyeball the bouncers to check our IDs
at every room of sharp-shirted boners
sniffing raras with skirts as high as stoners
with their endless Mum and Dad funds.
Daddy's little "dirt boxes" deflowered
during every night I never showed,
with every failed attempt to plunder
solved by a Sourz or a tactical chunder,
until eleven,
when everything shut,
but Bo's, The Drink and Cinderellas.

How they'd flight the alphas when they'd bring,
how they'd mock the homeless by Burger King,
a mating call for all the fellas
from our Lynx-effected lack of shame
and how tonight we're off the cocaine.

But for small town eighteen
and all that it seemed,

I lost my faith
in their hand-me-down dreams,
yet through all the strawpedos
and a little bad sex,
I'd always arise
to the cries in their eyes,
as I learnt to party with a frown
with the prettyboys of Gangster Town.

Their adulthood looked effortless,
as younger me had been,
in scruffy clothes
in Scruffy Murphy's,
where the bouncers were bruisers,
the bar was obscene
and the pints of pipe cleaner
drowned every last thought
for a pair of tenners
and a photocopy of my 'passport',
that taught us innocence was not to be trusted
on the day my dear old Scruffy's got busted,
but the prettyboys were unaware
of any other kind of care
and any time I'd hark on back,
my dear old Scruffy's came under attack.

I tried to copy how the prettyboys lived,
with every last fiver every cashpoint would give,
on semi alert for the tossers and tools
from the daily misery of secondary school
and wondering if anyone would ever understand
why their town was far from a wonderland,
just the same old streets of photocopied times
where it mattered whose Dads
earnt more than mine.

hand

I learnt those nights.
I learnt them well.
I learnt that Gangster Town was hell,
that small towns make big choices,
that small towns amplify small voices,
that small town misfits finish last,
that small towns trap you in their future
and your past.

Gangster Town,
where I was from.
Gangster Town,
where I didn't belong.
A town that, years ago, ceased to exist
when the prettyboys abandoned station,
leaving the night to a new generation
unaware of the ghost of a stranger called me,
who meets my eyes with a party frown
when I take a walk down Bridge Street
through the remnants of Gangster Town.

My ghost looks intently,
as I grow older,
at the former site
of the chip on my shoulder
that put my roots under secret duress
when they failed at his idea of success,
as if no other town had prettyboys
out-drinking their cares
in awful bars
and no other town
would have made me slate
the fate I found
in fused and fading convolutions
of teenage confusion.

But although I'm locked
to that party frown,
I clutch a key
to my small Surrey town,
to the nights behind
the Bridge Street walls
that built walls in my mind,
to how somewhere,
in all those hand-me-down dreams
I found everybody's dreams but mine.

A fallow frown,
copyright
of a little place
some teenagers
once called
Gangster Town.

feeds you.

About the Author

Martin Grey failed English at school, and was told by his English teacher that he would never be a writer. Based in Nottingham but originally from Guildford, he is a director of World Jam, a nonprofit for connecting communities through poetry and music, and a zine editor, event organiser and compere for DIY Poets, a Nottingham based spoken word collective.

He has performed extensively around the Midlands and as far afield as Berlin and Edinburgh Fringe, where he co-ran the spoken word show A DIY Poetry Fix in 2019. He won the 2018 Southwell Folk Festival slam and his work has been featured in Nottingham City of Literature, The Poetry Archive and MudPress Christmas zine.

He is a keen runner, sci-fi nerd, slightly ropey Spanish speaker, prefers tea to coffee and eats far too much cake. Sometimes he wonders if people keep mistaking him for the poet they actually wanted and are too polite to tell him, but he plans to keep going until he's rumbled.

The Prettyboys of Gangster Town is his first book. He hopes you enjoyed reading it as much as he enjoyed writing it.

Social Media:
@martin_grey_poet (Instagram)
@martingreypoet (Facebook)
@martingreypoet (YouTube)
www.worldjam.co.uk
www.martingreypoet.com

Thanks to @at.the.poetry for the photo.

About *Fly on the Wall Press*

A publisher with a conscience.
Publishing high quality anthologies on pressing issues,
chapbooks and poetry products, from exceptional poets around the globe.
Founded in 2018 by founding editor, Isabelle Kenyon.

Other publications:
Please Hear What I'm Not Saying
(February 2018. Anthology, profits to Mind.)
Persona Non Grata
(October 2018. Anthology, profits to Shelter and Crisis Aid UK.)
Bad Mommy / Stay Mommy by Elisabeth Horan
The Woman With An Owl Tattoo by Anne Walsh Donnelly
the sea refuses no river by Bethany Rivers
White Light White Peak by Simon Corble
Second Life by Karl Tearney
The Dogs of Humanity by Colin Dardis
Planet in Peril
(September 2019. Anthology, profits to WWF and The Climate Coalition.)
Small Press Publishing: The Dos and Don'ts by Isabelle Kenyon
Alcoholic Betty by Elisabeth Horan
Awakening by Sam Love
Grenade Genie by Tom McColl
House of Weeds by Amy Kean and Jack Wallington
No Home In This World by Kevin Crowe
The Goddess of Macau by Graeme Hall

Social Media:
@fly_press (Twitter)
@flyonthewall_poetry (Instagram)
@flyonthewallpoetry (Facebook)
www.flyonthewallpoetry.co.uk